Elisabetta Putini

A POMPEIAN NOTEBOOK

Discovering a Buried City with Stories and Games

Translated by Maureen B. Fant

Drawings by Cristina Neri

«L'ERMA» di BRETSCHNEIDER

Pompeii: Who, what, where

Pompeii is a small Italian city, located in the region of Campania, a few miles from the large city of Naples. It looks out on the sea and lies at the foot of a volcano, Mount Vesuvius. Today it is a modern city, spelled Pompei in Italian, a popular destination for scholars and tourists, who go there to visit the remains of the ancient city.

Almost 2000 years ago, a terrible eruption of the volcano Vesuvius completely buried the ancient city of Pompeii and killed every living thing in it.

But under that blanket of death, the city was preserved, almost as it was. Archaeologists who excavated it found not only bodies and objects but also inscriptions, houses, furniture, jewelry, and even food and fossilized plants. Analysis of the finds has made it possible to reconstruct the history of Pompeii up to that awful final day, that of the eruption, the 24th of August in the year AD 79.

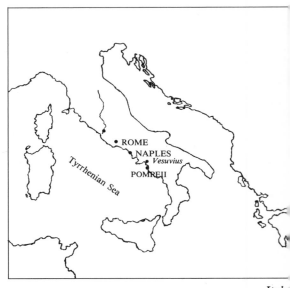

Italy

This "notebook" will tell you the story of that buried city. As you read, you will learn something, but you should also have some fun. You'll find curiosities, games, and a small map of the excavations that may come in handy one day when you visit Pompeii yourself.

CONTENTS

= games and activities

Pompeii: the final day (August 24, 79)

The pictures tell the story of the destruction of Pompeii. Use your imagination to color the figures.

It is almost noon. The Pompeians are going about their daily business in the buildings and streets. Then suddenly the sun grows dark. A suffocating heat makes the air unbreathable—too hot even for a day in late August ...

B-O-O-M! An ear-splitting noise shakes even the air itself. The ground trembles. The volcano called Vesuvius explodes and then seems to crumble into a hail of incandescent stones. A storm of small stones called lapilli falls on the city of Pompeii.

The houses fill with gas from the volcano. Ashes rain down and fill up every little crack, and make it impossible to move or even to see.

People rush screaming into the streets, trying to find refuge where they can. But the burning rain keeps falling, burying people, animals, things...

Their cries are stifled by the gas. For everyone, flight is impeded by the dark, by fear, by chaos caused by all the other people running away.

Some people still try to leave the city, to reach the sea. They hold roof tiles or pieces of wood over their heads like makeshift umbrellas to protect themselves.

Someone is trapped in his house and dies, asphyxiated by dense smoke. Other people try to fight their way out, protecting their heads with their arms.

Entire families are attacked by the lapilli. Men, women, and children are buried together.

A woman tries to save her valuables and grabs her heavy strongbox. But she is buried along with her coins and jewelry.

But the burning rain of ash won't stop. The level of debris rises to the windows of buildings, then even higher, past the roofs, until it covers everything. The city of Pompeii is dead.

From that day on, the site where Pompeii once stood becomes known as Civitas, later La Civita, the city without a name, the city that isn't there. But Pompeii was not the only victim of Vesuvius.

The nearby towns of Herculaneum and Stabiae were buried by a river of lava. Three days later, all the territory around Vesuvius was covered by white ash, showing no sign of life. It looked like the moon.

The first vulcanologist: a boy named Pliny

Pliny is only seventeen years old. He is a quiet boy who loves to read and to observe nature. His father is dead, but Pliny is very close to his mother and his uncle, Pliny the Elder, whose name he bears.

It is the end of August, AD 79, and Pliny is at Misenum, a few miles from Pompeii. His uncle-guardian is stationed here because he is admiral of the imperial Roman fleet.

Everything seems calm, but Pliny is restless: for several nights he has had trouble sleeping. He wakes up with a start. He is covered in sweat and very nervous. Maybe it's the heat, or maybe it's earth tremors, which are very common in the area of the Bay of Naples.

Then, on the 24th, something finally happens. At about 1 p.m., from his house Pliny sees a huge, mysterious cloud in the distance. Slowly it assumes the form of a giant pine tree. The cloud seems to come from a mountain, but only later will it be known that that mountain is Vesuvius. Pliny is shaken but curious.

His uncle sets boldly off for high ground, the better to observe the phenomenon. But the situation rapidly grows frightening, and people begin to notice the danger and ask for help. Without a moment's hesitation Pliny the Elder launches a rescue mission by sea, with himself in the lead. But the ashes mixed with pumice and pebbles blackened by the fire are already falling on the ships. Slowly evening falls, flames and gases are released from Vesuvius. There is a hail of lapilli. Everywhere, the air stinks of sulfur.

Pliny the Younger observes from afar. After his uncle left, he took refuge in his books, then had a bath and dinner and tried to sleep. But Misenum, too, suffers a violent earthquake. The sea seems to bend in half, and the cloud of smoke in the distance is lit by flashes of fire. Pliny and his mother leave the town and take refuge with the others on the beach, in the hope of being safe. All around them they hear the cries and wailing of desperate people.

Then slowly the inferno cools down and a pallid sun announces the new day. Only many hours later does the news reach Misenum that Pliny the Elder has died, asphyxiated by poison gas and ashes.

* * *

Twenty-five years later, in AD 104, Pliny the Younger writes two letters to his friend Tacitus, who is writing a history of Rome. The letters recount his uncle's death on the shore near Stabiae and describes his own feelings as an eyewitness to the terrible eruption that destroyed Pompeii, Herculaneum, and Stabiae.

These letters are the first written observation and description of a volcanic phenomenon, and so we can call Pliny the first *vulcanologist*.

Today vulcanology is the science that studies such phenomena and describes their phases. Even if it really dates back to Pliny, vulcanology as a true scientific discipline began only in the 19th century.

Vesuvius: short history of a volcano

Vesuvius is an active volcano. It is formed from two cones, one on top of the other. The outer cone, Mount Somma, is the older, and from inside its crater rises the large inner cone, Mount Vesuvius. Between the two cones, Somma and Vesuvius, lies a valley.

Vesuvius was formed after many successive eruptions. The lava materials that erupted from the central core or from lateral openings have solidified over time, creating a true volcanic mountain.

A volcano usually has a central crater at the summit and other, smaller craters, called adventive craters. An eruption can be one of two types: (1) lava only, without explosions, or (2) mixed, in which flows of lava alternate with explosions, during which small burning pieces of material, ashes, and lapilli are thrown out.

VOLCANO WITH ADVENTIVE CRATERS

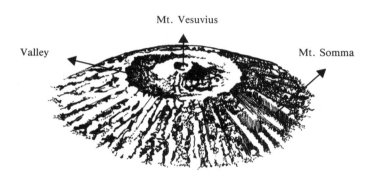

THE VOLCANO

Vesuvian eruptions are of the mixed type, with tremendous explosions. In Roman times, until 79, the volcano had been in a period of dormancy (rest) after thousands of years of activity. For the Romans it was just a large green mountain. It seems that nobody suspected that it was a volcano that could wake up at any moment!

The beginning of the new active phase was signaled, in the year AD 62, seventeen years before the great eruption, by a disastrous earthquake. Many centuries later, in 1621, another catastrophe occurred: lava from Vesuvius invaded the surrounding towns and took some 4000 lives.

From then on, almost all eruptions of Vesuvius have been characterized by this sequence of events: weak initial activity → increase in activity with explosions and lava flows → a maximum point → a rest period.

CONE VOLCANO

AND SIMPLE CRATER

Think and play

☐ Which of the following statements do you think is correct?

○ A vulcanologist repairs tires.
○ A vulcanologist is a scientist who observes, studies, and describes volcanic eruptions.
○ A vulcanologist is somebody who lives in a volcanic area.

☐ Read this ancient document:

"While the Senate was meeting in Rome, a messenger arrived all out of breath from Naples to bring news of the eruption of Etna and the destruction of Pompeii."

One little detail should tell you that the document is a fake. What?

☐ Three of the following four natural phenomena are often found in volcanic areas. Check the one that doesn't fit.

○ Geyser   ○ Solfatara   ○ Earthquake   ○ Waterfall

Excavations: the mysteries of the buried cities

Excavations to dig up the remains of Pompeii began just a few days after the destruction. But these mostly represented either looting or attempts to recover bodies and such valuables as could be most easily extracted from the rubble. We can imagine that it was the few survivors of the catastrophe, or the inhabitants of the neighboring cities, who attempted these early excavations.

Only toward the middle of the 1700s do true archaeological excavations begin to bring to light the remains of the lost city known as "Civita." After the first finds came to light, the city once again came to be called Pompeii. The discoveries followed one upon another at a rapid pace, and the fame of Pompeii and Herculaneum spread throughout Europe. Even kings—eager to possess the magnificent works of art and beautiful objects being found—offered large amounts of money to finance the digs.

In this way, Pompeii slowly got back its temples, villas, shops, and streets, and gradually began once again to look like the ancient city.

After 1861, with the unification of Italy, the digging became less a treasure hunt and more scientific. The new director of excavations, Giuseppe Fiorelli, launched this more organized work: he kept an excavation journal, divided the city into sectors, and gave every house an identification number. More than 500 men worked under him.

Fiorelli invented and introduced the sensational method of making plaster casts of the dead bodies, preserving exactly their form and position at the time of death.

During the eruption, the burning ashes covered the bodies, surrounding them completely, and then solidified around the bodies. This sort of sheath was then slowly emptied out as the flesh decomposed. Thus the skeleton was imprisoned in a sort of cavity, which, on the inside, maintained the forms of the body. Fiorelli's brilliant idea was to inject this cavity with small quantities of plaster to make a cast. When the plaster dried, the cast was carefully removed. These casts—in the exact form of the dying people and animals, some with mouths open in now-silent cries of pain or gesturing desperately—provide poignant testimony not only of the agony of death but of the clothes people wore and objects they used in life.

Fiorelli's system made it possible to discover many details until then unknown about daily life in Pompeii. Casts are still being made today, but thanks to a new material, a semitransparent resin, the modern casts reveal even more. You can see even the expression on their faces and the objects grasped in their hands as they died. And as you look at the victims of the tragedy thus preserved, you can not only imagine the drama of that moment but also feel like an eyewitness to a great historic event.

Pompeii: a few words about the city's history

About 600 years before the birth of Christ, Pompeii was founded by the Opici, an ancient people of southern Italy. It was only a small village, and the people lived simply by fishing and farming. They may have already begun doing a bit of trading, perhaps barter, with the neighboring cities of Cumae and Nola.

Its excellent location on the sea was very attractive to two other peoples who were active in the region, colonizing and trading. These were the Greeks and the Etruscans, and they fought over Pompeii, until the Greeks finally prevailed, in the 5th century BC.

Then, toward the end of that century, another group arrived, the Samnities from the mountains inland. They occupied the rich plains around Capua, and came to be called "Campani." They made repeated forays into the region that still today bears their name, Campania. Even Pompeii (whose inhabitants were by this time now known as Oscans) was eventually occupied.

The citizens of Pompeii began to construct imposing fortifications to protect the city from further invasions: a double circuit of wall, with earth between the two walls, and large rectangular towers and eight gates. Outside the walls, the cemeteries (called necropolises, from the Greek for "city of the dead") began to grow. During the Samnite period (which is how archaeologists and historians define this time in the city's history) the major streets were put in, and new quarters were built with the ordered geometry of Greek architectural models.

Meanwhile, north of Pompeii, the city of Rome was expanding its power and influence in Italy. Near the end of the 4th century BC, the Romans reached Pompeii and things began to change: Pompeii and other Campanian cities became allies of Rome and swore loyalty to her. Some two centuries later, between 91 and 87 BC, Rome's Italian allies attempted to rebel. This war between Rome and the allies is known as the Social War. Under the command of Lucius Cornelius Sulla the Roman forces occupied Pompeii, in 89 BC, after a long siege.

This was the beginning of a long and peaceful time for Pompeii as a Roman colony named Cornelia (after Sulla's family name) Veneria (for the goddess Venus). It was a good arrangement both for the Romans and for the Pompeian merchants who began large-scale trade, exporting and importing products from all the Romanized lands. The enormous prosperity that followed was too good to last.

But when disaster struck, it was not at the hand of an enemy in war. It came from nature. In the year 62 BC a violent earthquake struck Pompeii. The inhabitants worked hard to repair and rebuild, but they had not yet finished when the volcano suddenly awoke.

Stories of daily life

What was life like in Pompeii?
Let's try to follow the day of a typical, rather well-off family that lives in downtown Roman Pompeii.

The father, whose name is Antonius, is the owner of a snack bar (*thermopolium*), with a counter facing the street. His place is known throughout the city, and he does a good business, especially on market days. It is located not far from the *macellum*, the major market of Pompeii, where meat, fish, fruit, and grains are sold. Antonius, who is a very hard worker, is one of the first to open up early in the morning. He fills his beautiful clay amphoras, which are set into the counter, and displays the wine goblets on a marble shelf. He prepares olives, cheeses, salamis. He lines up the cooked dishes on the hot table. Antonius loves his shop. He knows that many customers come because they know it's clean. Only once in a very great while do they find some bug or other floating in the barley soup.

Come on! It's seven in the morning and everything's ready. Antonius has already put some bronze coins (called *asses*) into his cash box, but he needs a lot more of them to keep a family like his! However, today is election day and he's expecting a good crowd. That's what Antonius is thinking as the city wakes up.

The loud clackety-clack of wagons and carts begins to die down, because traffic is prohibited on the main streets during the day. But there's plenty of noise and confusion anyway. The side streets fill up with busy people coming and going and with porters, hawkers, and artisans starting the day's work. On the sidewalk, barefoot toddlers play a game with nutshells, while the older children imitate grownups and use real dice. Little girls cuddle their dolls made of wax. But for everybody it's almost school time. Well, not for everybody. Only the children of the wealthier families go to school.

Thermopolium of Antonius

11

Septimius, age 11, is Antonius' son. He has light hair and tan skin. He wears a short tunic and sandals (*soleae*) laced high. He's running as fast as he can down Forum Street because he is, as always, late for school. But everything distracts him! As he looks around, he trips on a big slab of paving stone. Oh, no! All his school things land in the mud! His two rolls of papyrus, his wax tablet and his beautiful sharp new styluses! Septimius hurriedly gathers everything up and tries to clean up as best he can. Then he puts the dirtied papyrus and the stylus, sharp no longer, back in his round schoolbag (*capsa*). Oh, well! The boy is fascinated by the comings and goings in the Forum and quickly forgets the incident—and his tardiness. Look, he's now in the large pedestrian island and here he feels important too! The Forum seems like a "little Rome"—that's what his Greek teacher (strict, yes, but a very learned man) called it. This is the center of the political, social, and religious life of Pompeii. Just about everything important that happens in the city takes place in one of the buildings of the huge square known in every ancient Roman city as the forum.

Septimius' curiosity is now attracted by the Comitium, a large marble-covered building, where a large crowd of people is gathering. Who knows why? Of course! It's election day, thinks the boy, and all the men are going to vote! Everywhere, on the walls of the city, appear electoral notices, some of them rather funny. For example, one says "Vote for Lucius, a very honest man! (signed) The Guild of Thieves."

It just doesn't seem like a school day today, thinks Septimius as he walks in front of the Basilica, the law court. But then he gives a little shiver as the thinks of his own judges—his teacher, his father, his mother. They'd never forgive him for playing hooky. He's risking a bout with the *ferula*, the cane used to punish lazy pupils. What should he do?

What Septimius takes to school:

— round schoolbag *(capsa)*
— papyrus
— wax tablet
— styluses
— pen

While Septimius is tormented by doubt, let us leave the Forum, and its electoral fever, and go to the house of Domitilla, Antonius' wife. Here, Domitilla and Livia, her elder daughter, age 18, are starting their day. Like all Pompeian women, they are quite free and certainly do not spend their day shut up in the house! You can meet them strolling in the street, at the market, the Forum, calling on their friends. They attend meetings and banquets. But there's plenty of work to do at home.

The *domus*, or house, where Antonius and Domitilla live is not as roomy and elegant as some more patrician houses, but it's still a very nice house. It has a rather large *atrium*, which serves as a central courtyard, with its fine pool for collecting rainwater (*impluvium*); around it are arranged the rooms: the dining room (*triclinium*), the bedrooms (*cubicula*), the kitchen, and the storerooms. Of course, there is also the little shrine to the Lares, the household gods who protect the family. What is, however, missing, in Domitilla's opinion, is a beautiful garden at the back, perhaps with a columned portico (*peristylium*). That's the secret dream of the lady of the house, but we all have to make do. The old slave, Drusa, whom the family loves, begins to do the housework, sweeping the refuse out into the street, as she does every morning. Livia, too, helps out in the house. She particularly enjoys fooling around in the kitchen, and she's not bad at it either. She bakes rolls kneaded with ricotta (*libum*) and makes dishes that Antonius sells in his *thermopolium*—olive pies, soups made of grains. At eight in the morning the house already smells of spices and freshly baked bread.

Meanwhile, Domitilla has completed her toilette, with special attention to her hair. Then a quick round of housework, which is not too difficult because there's really not much furniture in the house. But then she has to think of the family's meals. Today it's Domitilla's turn to shop, but she's always happy to go out since she sees her friends and can stop for a chat. The cost of living has certainly gone up! As usual, 30 *asses* won't be enough: 8 for bread, 2 for wine, 2 for cheese, 5 for oil and then ... all the rest! That's what Domitilla thinks on her way to the market.

Livia goes out right after her mother and takes the prepared foods to her father's shop. At noon the women are home to eat a quick meal (a little cheese, an onion, some fruit) and then take up their favorite pastimes. Livia paints, Domitilla works at her loom, and old Drusa snores in her room.

At about the ninth hour (three in the afternoon) Septimius comes home (from school?). Antonius, tired and hungry, arrives a bit later. It is late afternoon and the whole family eats the main meal (*coena*) together in the *triclinium*, lying on special dining couches. Everyone seems to have a good appetite.

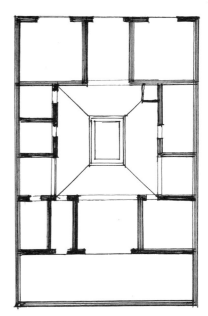
Plan of Antonius and Domitilla's house

Atrium of a patrician house

Triclinium

13

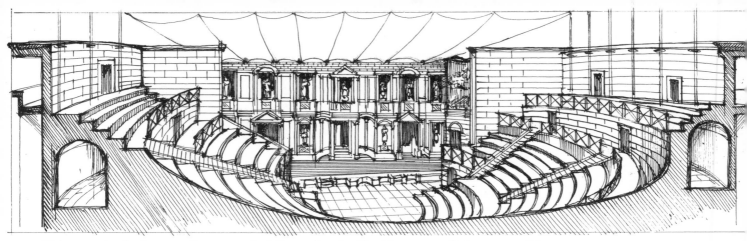

Not every day is the same for our typical Pompeian family. There are religious occasions, entertainment, the baths, and more.

Antonius often goes to the baths to relax after a hard day's work. He chats with his friends, gets a little exercise in the open air and has a sauna in the *sudatorium*, then a hot, relaxing bath in the *caldarium* and a quick plunge in the icy *frigidarium*. After a massage, he's back in shape and the fatigue melts away. Domitilla is happy to go along with him, but, please, no exercise!

On very special days, the family might go to the theater.

Antonius prefers the large open-air theater, where the shows include mimes and uproarious Atellan farces, which are a bit too coarse for the children. So Domitilla insists on going to the Odeon, the small covered theater, where they hear music and poetry readings. But nothing can beat the excitement of the Amphitheater: battles between gladiators, men against wild animals! Yes, it's true, the shows are a little gory, but the spectators certainly seem to enjoy themselves.

Religious observances are frequent, in the home and outside. Among the domestic rites, that at the *lararium* holds first place. Every day Antonius, surrounded by his family, including the slave Drusa, worships the gods who protect the house: the two Lares and the three major gods Hercules, Bacchus, and Venus. He asks them for good fortune, prosperity and, why not?, some vintage wine.

The three even more powerful gods Jupiter, Juno, and Minerva demand worship too. In the Forum, where the great Temple of Jupiter is located dominating the square, the three statues can be seen between the columns and command respect. They are the official patron gods of Rome, and only the priests can perform the rites in their honor. Many Pompeians worship Isis, the Egyptian goddess, whose worship is a foreign import. Sometimes Livia participates in the ceremony of the lustral water that takes place every day, at 2.30 p.m. on the dot. Since she's such a fanatic for the cult of Isis, once a year, on March 5, she drags the whole family to the great festival in honor of the goddess, who protects sailors (*Navigium Isidis*).

There's no escaping the gods because religion at Pompeii is such an important part of the daily life of every typical family.

Odeon

Lararium

The absent-minded artist

Here are portraits of Antonius, Livia, and Domitilla. But somebody's missing. Our painter is very absent-minded. Why don't you try to help him?

Map of Pompeii

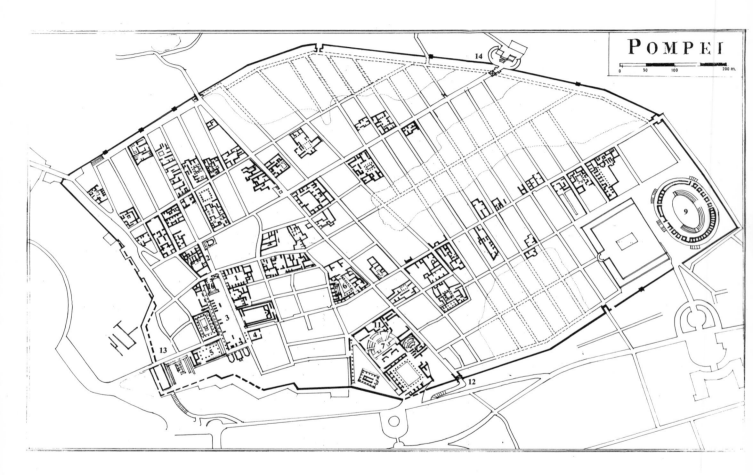

1. Macellum   2. Forum Street   3. Forum   4. Comitium   5. Basilica   6. A public bath   7. Theater   8. Odeon
9. Amphitheater   10. Temple of Jupiter   11. Temple of Isis   12. Stabian Gate   13. Marine Gate   14. Nola Gate

Look and play

1. Look at the map of Pompeii on page 16 and find the places mentioned in "Stories of daily life" (pages 11 to 14).

2. Look carefully the map of Pompeii: where would you place each of these people?

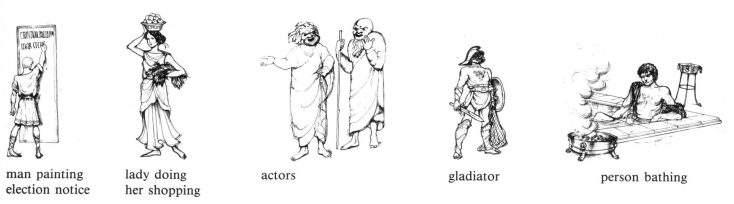

man painting
election notice

lady doing
her shopping

actors

gladiator

person bathing

3. We are in the "House of the Gilded Cupids," one of Pompeii's most elegant houses. Can you match objects and furnishings with their respective rooms? Fill in the blank with the letter corresponding to the correct picture.

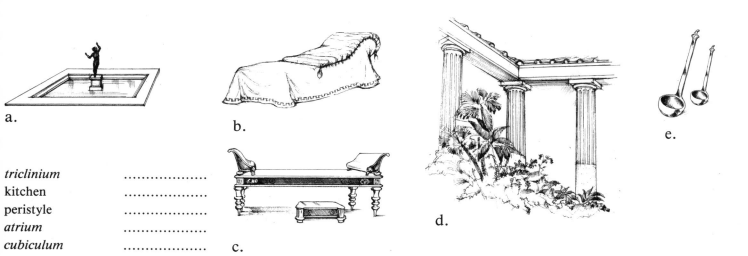

a.

b.

triclinium . . . .

kitchen . . . .

peristyle . . . .

atrium . . . .

cubiculum . . . .

c.

d.

e.

The tired archaeologist

The archaeologist Camilla goes to Pompeii to excavate. She is walking and carrying a heavy bag. Along the road she decides to jettison three things because she is just too tired to go on. Here's what she's carrying. What do you think she could safely do without?

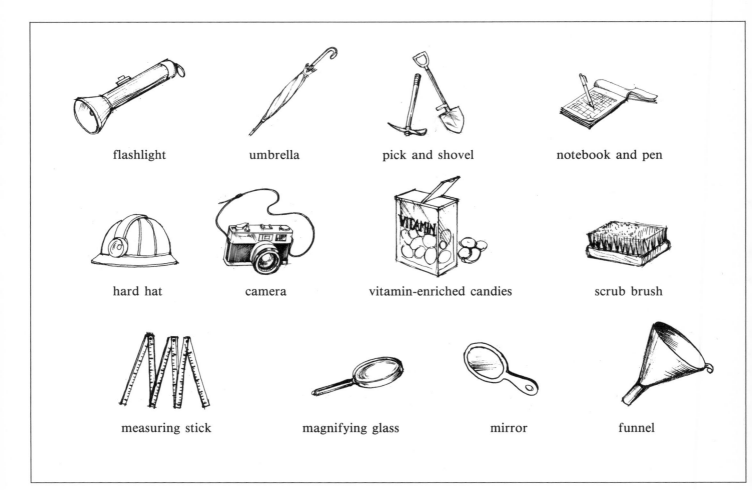

flashlight   umbrella   pick and shovel   notebook and pen

hard hat   camera   vitamin-enriched candies   scrub brush

measuring stick   magnifying glass   mirror   funnel

18

Archaeological treasure hunt

Look at the map on page 16 and go with Camilla on this extraordinary adventure.

Camilla the archaeologist, more exhausted than ever, begins to dig. She finds an ancient Latin inscription which says: "If you want to find a treasure, I'll give you a clue: go to the gate of the *wet blue*." Where should Camilla go?

Write the map reference number next to your answer.

- a. To the Nola Gate
- b. To the Stabian Gate
- c. To the Marine Gate

Good girl, Camilla! She found the right gate. To work!

Two hours later, another inscription gives Camilla the second clue: "Look for the secret in the place of *cabbages and cods.*" Camilla seems confused, but then starts off confidently for—where?

- a. Comitium
- b. Macellum
- c. Amphitheater

Good, Camilla is right on target! Here she digs again and finds another clue: it's the base of a column and something is inscribed on it: "Go to the place where *hot water becomes lukewarm and then freezing.*" Camilla hesitates. What is this mysterious place?

- a. A public bath
- b. Temple of Isis
- c. Forum

She is near the end of her search and feeling triumphant. But where's the treasure? All of a sudden Camilla sees Gigi, her assistant and something of a joker, on his way over, chuckling slyly. Oh no! It was all a joke! Gigi, of all people, had planted the false archaeological "clues." Poor Camilla, after all that work, will just have to be happy with an ice cream. And you? Add up all the numbers next to your answers and check the solution printed upside down at the bottom of the page. If your number is the same, you deserve a certificate as a "friend of archaeology." Well done!

Solution: 13 + 1 + 6 = 20

A very easy recipe

Here's a special snack you can make for your friends—Pompeian sweets that are delicious and very easy to make. They taste a little like cheesecake.

Pompeian balls

> 200 g (7 oz) fresh, white, unsalted cheese (like ricotta)
> 20 unsalted almonds, peeled and chopped
> 1 egg yolk
> 3 tablespoons honey
> 6 or 7 dry, sweet cookies

Put the cheese in a bowl and add the egg yolk, the honey, and the chopped almonds. Mix well. With slightly wet (and very clean!) hands, form lots of little balls. Put the cookies between two sheets of waxed paper and roll with a rolling pin, or pound with a meat tenderizer, until they are pulverized. Then roll the cheese balls in the cookie crumbs and arrange the little balls neatly on a serving plate. Insert a toothpick in each ball and put the plate in the freezer for about an hour. Garnish with candied fruit.

Let's play with coins

As a Roman colony, Pompeii, uses Roman money.
Here are the denominations:

— *Aurei*   (gold coins)   1 *aureus* = 25 *denarii*
— *Denarii* (silver coins)   1 *denarius* = 4 *sesterces*
— *Sestertii* (bronze coins) 1 *sestertius* (sesterce, in English) = 4 *asses*
— *Asses*   (bronze coins)   The *as* is the minimum value. It is subdivided into
                              fractions (e.g., *semis*, or half-*as*).

Problem:

Domitilla is going shopping because she has guests for
dinner. In her purse are 4 *denarii* and 3 sesterces. The
grocer wants 60 *asses*. How much money will she have
left for the perfume shop?

Pairs: solve the problem and read your profile

Here is a group of important objects found in Pompeii. Can you complete the caption and put it under the right picture?

A	B	C	D

1 - Small .... made of clay used in homes for religious rites. Probably used to burn incense and perfume.

2 - Bronze vessel resting on three lion's .... : used to heat beverages ("samovar"). A device inside (siphon), in which burning coal was placed, permitted heating the liquid, which was poured through the small .... in the upper part of the object.

3 - Bronze statuette depicting a dancing ....s were considered household gods: they protected the .... and the family. In many Pompeian houses there were *lararia*, shrines or small altars, for conducting the daily religious rites.

4 - A right .... made of bronze making a gesture of blessing. The .... can be considered an amulet: it was believed that it would protect the mother and child depicted on it.

Read your profile

Check the upside-down solution on page 22, then give yourself 3 points for every correct match.

— 12 to 9 points:

You are active, attentive, and perceptive. You are a good observer and have a good aesthetic sense and good intuition. Bravo!

— 6 to 3 points:

You are lively, sociable, and a bit of a dreamer. Sometimes you find it difficult to concentrate because your imagination wanders. When you decide to do something, you do it your way.

— 3 to 0 points:

Impossible! You must have been thinking about something else! Or maybe you're waiting for something really important to capture your attention. Relax, and then try again.

1ª ristampa aprile 2000

ISBN 88-7062-906-6

Stampa: Tipograf Srl - Via C. Morin, 26/A - Roma